THE MOST COMPLETE BEETHOVEN PIANO SOLOS
Books I & II In One Volume

A Comprehensive Collection Of His World Famous Works

Bagatelles

Contra-Dances

Rondos

Sonatinas

Sonatas

Popular Short Piano Pieces

IN THEIR ORIGINAL FORM

Compiled By
ALEXANDER SHEALY

LUDWIG VAN BEETHOVEN

BORN BONN, GERMANY, DECEMBER 16, 1770
DIED VIENNA, AUSTRIA, MARCH 26, 1827

Beethoven composed music ever since he was a child. He was only 13 when his early compositions were published. At 22, he settled in Vienna, where he gained fame for his exceptional talent at the piano and his extraordinary ability in composing and improvising while performing. He had his "lean years" financially for some years at a time, but for the most part did very well. His works were good sellers and provided him with a comfortable livelihood. He never married — though he dedicated some of his works to a certain "immortal beloved".

When Beethoven was a little over 30, he began to develop ear trouble, which gradually grew worse through the years, until at 50, he was almost totally deaf. Even then, he was able to hear music within himself and this shocking development hindered but did not destroy his creativeness.

Here indeed was the giant of composers! Lasting through the centuries, and with no diminution of popularity, the world has inherited from him a wealth of beautiful piano pieces (the ever popular MINUET IN G and FUER ELISE and many others), a series of symphonies (of which the 5th, 7th and 9th are in the standard repertory of every concert orchestra), the revolutionary EROICA SYMPHONY, works of deep religious feeling, like the MISSA SOLEMNIS, the opera FIDELIO, string quartets, 32 remarkably original and beautiful sonatas (of which the MOONLIGHT SONATA and the SONATA PATHETIQUE are outstanding examples), the VIOLIN CONCERTO, and many other great works.

Indeed a rich inheritance!

Contents

BEETHOVEN AT AGE 15

HOUSE IN BONN, GERMANY
(BIRTHPLACE OF BEETHOVEN)

SONATINA IN G

LUDWIG VAN BEETHOVEN

ROMANZA
Allegretto

SONATINA IN F

LUDWIG VAN BEETHOVEN

Allegro assai

RONDO
Allegro

LUDWIG VAN BEETHOVEN - AT AGE 31

SONATE

für Piano-Forte und Violin.

Sr. Kaiserl. Hoheit dem durchlauchtigsten Prinzen

RUDOLPH

ERZHERZOG von OESTERREICH &c.&c.

in tiefer Ehrfurcht zugeeignet

von

Ludwig van Beethoven-

●●● 96tes Werk ●●●

N° 2581.
Preis

Eigenthum der Verleger.

WIEN
bei S. A. Steiner und Comp.

RAGE OVER A LOST PENNY

(RONDO A CAPRICCIO)

LUDWIG VAN BEETHOVEN
Opus 129

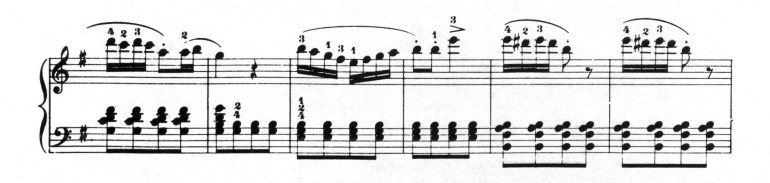

EDITORIAL NOTE:

This classic humoresque of Beethoven's was found among the composer's manuscripts after his death. The opus number was assigned by the publisher.

(a) The choice of the *major mode* of the *relative mi-nor* key (or of the minor third below) for this episode, is, in our opinion, a new proof that this work belongs to the later creative period. In an earlier period, the author would assuredly have chosen E♭ major instead of E

major. Beethoven did not cultivate the remoter key-rela-tionships until a later period; e. g., in the first movements of Op. 97 and Op 106.

(b) This salutation to the coming Mendelssohn must be played with the greatest possible elasticity of touch

(a) Here the player should recall the genesis of this humoresque. The original heading, in the Master's hand, reads: "Rage over the lost Groschen, vented in a Caprice." In this passage one can almost see the papers flying helter-skelter from the table, in the hasty search after the lost object. Assuredly, the almighty genius of this master might have written an *opera buffa,* had he found an outward or inward occasion for so doing.

(a) Notice the modulatory progressions:

This is something different from the everyday reverse progression from A♭ to D, and is a further support for our chronological opinion. In this connection we are reminded of an analogous example in the C major Mass, op. 86, where Beethoven, in a similar manner (by inverting a commonplace progression,) discovered a new modulatory succession of such imposing boldness, that no composer has since then dared to imitate it.

(a) As we shall meet with several more "thunderstorms" in the course of this piece, it is advisable to be chary in employing the device of tempo-acceleration in their representation, so that a continued intensification may be possible. For this reason, the editor plays this episode quite strictly (though not rigidly) in the principal tempo, and chiefly employs changes in dynamic shading for the animation of the delivery, always permitting a slight decrescendo in the descending figuration in either hand (i.e., alternately), and playing the ascending figuration crescendo.

The use of the pedal is permitted — so far, of course, as it does not conflict with purity of harmony.

(b) Considering that, if the Rondo had been published during the author's lifetime, he would certainly have revised it beforehand, we propose the following alteration of the bass, which appears calculated to obviate the lameness inherent in the text as it stands:

By letting the left hand take the beginning of the long scale in the right hand, as shown here in the three last notes, the flow of the right-hand part will not be interrupted by the leap of the twelfth.

(a) The independence of the several parts in these melodic and rhythmic imitations, which lends euphony to otherwise harsh dissonances (e. g., in the ninth and tenth measures), must bring renewed conviction to every thoughtful student of Beethoven, that this is not a work of the composer's youth.

(b) Always separate the two eighth-notes from the following quarter-note; but, of course, without making the intention too marked.

(a) This passage is to be played with the most tender touch, and yet with a (gnome-like) bustling and agility corresponding, in its way, to the characteristic "venting of rage" announced by the composer

(a) Take care not to play fortissimo too early; the demands of the succeeding pages on the player's physical powers are very considerable.

wearied fingers:

(b) As the movement must not drag, under any circumstances, the editor suggests the following facilitation for

the assisting left hand must, of course, carry out its fragmentary participation in the figure with the lightest touch.

(a) For the culmination of the paroxysm, beginning here, the tempo of the commencement must be almost doubled.

(b) The desideratum here is not so much simple material power, as a certain kind of staccato touch which we should call "scintillating."

(c) The melodic thread (i. e., the rhythmic phrasing) ought to be brought out with extreme clearness: The Master could not have betrayed the period, in which his last piano humoresque was written, more distinctly, than in this modulation.

(a) For swiftness of movement (which must, of course, be greatly moderated in comparison with the preceding) is now again to be substituted extreme power (combined with lightness — the chords thrown off with uplifted hand).

(a) The preceding canon, in which exhausted rage gradually begins to yield to returning self-possession, should not yet be moderated as to tempo, although it must be played without any unrestfulness. Only now has reflexion regained its sway; the direction *moderato,* given by us, is necessary for technical reasons as well, because this passage, played with most limpid transparency, is one of the most difficult in the piece, and absolutely un-playable with any other than our "excogitated" fingering.

(b) Do not confound (G as suspension of the leading-note in the dominant chord) with (F♯ as changing-note to the tonic, in the triad). This, again, is a refinement of the last period.

SONATA FACILE

(Opus 49, No. 1)

Abbreviations: M. T., signifies Main Theme; S. T., Sub Theme; Cl. T., Closing Theme; D. G., Development-group; R., Return; Tr., Transition; Md. T., Mid-Theme; Ep., Episode; App., Appendix.

L. van BEETHOVEN.

a) *mfp* signifies: the first note *mf*, the following ones *p*.

b) With the comma we indicate places where the player must perceptibly mark the end of a rhythmic group or section, by lifting the last note just before its time-value expires, although the composer wrote no rest.

c)

d) The left hand more subdued than the right, but still accenting the first of each pair of 16th-notes (i. e.: the bass notes proper) somewhat more than the second.

e)

f) Here and in the next measure the left hand should accent only the first note in each group of 16th-notes somewhat more than the others, but in all cases less than the soprano.

g) As at d.)

h) In these three measures as at f.)

29

a) As at (f) on the preceding Page.

b) ≡

c) The left hand here again more subdued than the right.

d) As at (a).

e) In these twelve measures the first and third notes in each group of 16th notes should be made somewhat more prominent than the other notes, yet always in subordination to the melody, excepting the tones marked >.

a) From here through the next 6 measures the left hand, having the melody, should predominate over the right, and, where it has 2 tones, chiefly accentuate the higher one.

b) As on first Page.

c) The next 5 measures as on first Page.

d) Doubtless literally meant neither for ♪♪♪♪♪ nor for: ♪♪♪♪♪ but ♪♪♪♪♪

e) This and the following turns again as on first Page.

f) From here onward as on second Page.

a)

b) **Proceed only after a rest.**

a) In these groups of 16th-notes, accent each first note slightly more than the 5 following, while subordinating all to the soprano. These same accented notes, too, (except in the fourth measure) should be held down during the second 16th-note.

b) Also subordinate this accompaniment, but accent the first note of each triplet, as the bass note proper, trifle more than the other two.

a) ⸨music example⸩

b) Here, of course, only the first eighth-note in each measure should be accented.

a) From here up to the *ff* discreetly subordinate the left hand throughout (also in the repetitions of the fundamental tone.
b) Let the *ff* enter abruptly with the fourth eighth-note, without any previous *crescendo*.

SONATA FACILE

(Opus 49, No. 2)

LUDWIG VAN BEETHOVEN

Allegro ma non troppo ♩= 104

Tempo di Menuette.

TURKISH MARCH
(FROM "THE RUINS OF ATHENS")

LUDWIG VAN BEETHOVEN

FUER ELISE
(ALBUM LEAF)

LUDWIG VAN BEETHOVEN

Poco moto

ECOSSAISES IN E FLAT

LUDWIG VAN BEETHOVEN

SIX VARIATIONS

(ON THEME OF DUET FROM THE OPERA
"LA MOLINARA" BY GIOVANNI PAISIELLO)
NEL COR PIU NON MI SENTO

LUDWIG VAN BEETHOVEN

Poco allegretto

Theme

Var. I.

Var. II.

Var. III.

Tranquillo

Var. IV.

Poco piú animato

Var. VI.

SIX VARIATIONS

(On A Swiss Song)

LUDWIG VAN BEETHOVEN

CONTRA-DANCE No. 1

LUDWIG VAN BEETHOVEN

CONTRA-DANCE No. 2

LUDWIG VAN BEETHOVEN

MINUET IN G

LUDWIG VAN BEETHOVEN

GERTRUDE'S DREAM WALTZ

LUDWIG VAN BEETHOVEN

VICTORY THEME
(FROM "FIFTH SYMPHONY")

LUDWIG VAN BEETHOVEN

Poco allegro

SONATINA
(Opus 79)

LUDWIG VAN BEETHOVEN

Presto alla tedesca

MONUMENT TO BEETHOVEN - VIENNA

BAGATELLE

(No. 1 of "Seven Bagatelles", Opus 33)

Andante grazioso, quasi allegretto (♩.= 56). LUDWIG VAN BEETHOVEN

*Bring out this left hand melody.

BAGATELLE

(No. 2 of "Seven Bagatelles", Opus 33)

LUDWIG VAN BEETHOVEN

Scherzo (Allegro)

Minore (Trio I)

Coda.

BAGATELLE

(No. 3 of "Seven Bagatelles", Opus 33)

LUDWIG VAN BEETHOVEN

Allegretto

BAGATELLE

(No. 4 of "Seven Bagatelles", Opus 33)

Andante (♩ = 52.)

LUDWIG VAN BEETHOVEN

* Bring out the upper part in the left hand.

BAGATELLE

(No. 5 of "Seven Bagatelles", Opus 33)

LUDWIG VAN BEETHOVEN

Allegro ma non troppo

BAGATELLE

(No. 6 of "Seven Bagatelles", Opus 33)

LUDWIG VAN BEETHOVEN

Allegretto quasi andante.
Con una certa expressione parlante.

BAGATELLE

(No. 7 of "Seven Bagatelles", Opus 33)

LUDWIG VAN BEETHOVEN

LUDWIG VAN BEETHOVEN - The Composer's Grandfather

RONDO IN C

LUDWIG VAN BEETHOVEN

Moderato e grazioso M.M. ♩ = 96.

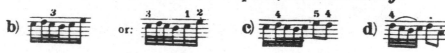

a) Abbreviation: (Principal subject, {Transition, {Subordinate subject, {Re-transition.
a) Abkürzungen: HS. bedeuted Hauptsatz, ÜG. Uebergang, SS. {Seitensatz, R G. {Rückgang.

a) *mp* a little louder than *piano*, and softer than *mf*.

a) This embellishment (as in a similar case in the first movement of Sonata, Op. 2, No. 3.) obviously not to be rendered literally but indicates only that the passage of 16ths is to be ornamented with appoggiatura, thus:

a) *calando*, meaning strictly the same as *diminuendo*, signifies here and generally, moreover, a gradual but not marked slackening of the *tempo*. ___ b) In this Quintuplet play the first two notes as 16ths, the remaining three as a triplet of 16ths.

a) Continue, after the hold, without **any break**.

a) This appoggiatura, as corresponding to the G in the preceding measure, should be played *before* the third beat, yet shorter than a 16th, say like a 32d.

ADIEU TO THE PIANO

LUDWIG VAN BEETHOVEN

Moderato, con molta espressione

TRIO

Dedicated to the Countess Giulietta Guicciardi

MOONLIGHT SONATA

(SONATA QUASI UNA FANTASIA)

Sonata No. 14, Opus 27, No. 2
Composed in 1802

LUDWIG van BEETHOVEN

a)   Use pedal with each bass note.   *)   No pedal.

b)   Strike both notes together, but stronger on upper note.

c)   PT: Principal Theme   ST: Secondary Theme   D: Development   Cl: Close or Ending

a) Bring out this principal theme a little, with the left hand.

Presto Agitato (♩=72.) (♩= 88, Von Bülow.)

a) **Play the first of these two chords with a strong accent but let the second be struck lightly, like a rebound of the hands from the keys.**

SONATA PATHETIQUE
(Opus 13)

LUDWIG VAN BEETHOVEN

Introduction.
Grave.

PIANO

attacca subito il Allegro.

Allegro di molto e con brio

Tempo I

Allegro molto e con brio

Adagio cantabile

SONATA APPASSIONATA

(Opus 57)

Editorial comments by
Hans Von Bulow
(1899)

LUDWIG VAN BEETHOVEN

a!) Execute the trill with appoggiatura as follows:

a) A player unable to perform this difficult passage with the requisite force and virtuosity, will do well to divide it between the hands, e. g.

b) An observance of the prescribed accentuation of the four counts (alternately in both hands) is absolutely essential to prevent metrical confusion in the syncopations.

c) By employing two fingers (1 and 2) on the same key, its exact repetition will be insured.

a) Without keen insight into the Master's thematic work, without a clear understanding of the process of the arising and passing-away of the several motives, an intelligent and intelligible interpretation of his works is impossible. As detailed analysis would swell this instructive edition to an "unpractical" bulk, and oral instruction by the teacher being, moreover, far more fruitful of good than written treatises, the Editor must content himself with occasional hints, leaving their exploitation to practical teaching. Take note, just here, of the melodic "passing-away," more particularly from the rhythmic point of view:

A. Rhythmical diminution.   B. Melodic disappearance of the descending second.

b) While observing the exact rhythmic precision demanded by the correct interpretation of this melody, which arises from the inversion of the first motive, be very careful to play the intermediate 16th-notes without over-sharp emphasis, an avoidance of which ought never, on the other hand, to lead to indistinctness.

a) The melody is not to be conceived simply as: but thus: so that the rhythmic pulsation may be duly brought out.

a) The melody lies in the lower part, and reads thus:

b) Do not bring in the fluttering figure in the right hand too soon; it should be taken as a kind **of** *auftakt* to the following chords in the left hand. The player is expressly cautioned to avoid the **a**-mateurish inclination to place the *sforzato* on the second beat instead of the fourth — a fault of very frequent occurrence.

c) For this and the following trills, compare the first Notes to this **Sonata**.

a) In the left hand, accent the second and fourth beats: ♪ properly ♪ From this opposition to the right-hand part there results a rhythmic polyphony in keeping with the passionate character of the whole episode.

Imagine, too, that in ♪ there is hidden a latent allusion to the motive ♪

a) The regular marking of the held tone A♭ as a quarter-note must not be taken literally, because the clearness of the movement in eighth-notes would then necessarily suffer, but is to be considered as a redundancy of the ruling expression-mark, urging the player to as full a *"vibrato"* as possible.

b) Here the composer doubtless forgot to write the *diminuendo*-sign for the last beat. A "slavish" observance of the abrupt change from *forte* to *piano*, which we have advocated everywhere else, especially when first studying the Master's works, (and desiring, as we do, the employment of this shading in the art of interpretation only in a good sense,) would necessarily break the continuity with the following measure and lead to unintelligibility. On the other hand,

c) the sudden entrance of the *piano* on the fourth beat is to be executed very literally; an imperceptible breathing-space, such as the comma calls for in speaking, is of course not merely allowable in similar cases, but absolutely essential.

a) Even if, generally speaking, an acceleration of tempo conjoined with an increase of force is more apt to weaken than to enhance the energy of expression, it appears to the Editor that here a simultaneous employment of both these means of intensification is altogether admissible,—that the effect of a heaven-storming culmination is æsthetically justified.

b) More virtuosity than is commonly supposed is demanded for the representation of this elemental thunderstorm. The rising and falling, python-like writhings of the bass passage from ♮ to ♮ and back into the lowermost depths, require most energetic accentuation, to bring out the lines of the melodic contours with the necessary clearness.

a) The doublings in the octave in the 4 following measures appears to us to be a facilitation, particularly after the player has fully recognized the difficulty of avoiding all harshness in the touch while putting forth his full strength. According to the individual make of the arms, the player will cross the left over or under the right.

b) The Editor plays the octaves at the re-entry of the principal theme with the unchanging fingering $\frac{5}{1}$, an immovable stretch of the fingers, and a downward inclination of the palm; as the use of the fourth finger on the black keys easily leads to a too early lifting of the thumb.

a) The transference of the chord on the strong beat from the right hand to the left will further the accentuation of the following syncopation.

The tempo-marks added by the Editor, *"quasi accel."* and *"quasi rit."*, must of course not lead to exaggeration.

a¹) The player is again reminded, that all trills should be begun on the higher auxiliary, which latter must precisely coincide with the change of the other parts on the beat. Consequently, at

b) the sharp dissonance resulting etc., is entirely conformable to the composer's intention.

a) At the risk of being accused of dealing in trifles — though for that matter every trifle is of high import-
ance in studying the interpretation of our great masters' works — the Editor feels constrained to express de-
cided doubts as to the correctness of the correction, i.e., simplification, which is in a degree sanctioned by
the new Härtel edition, of the reading found in earlier editions of the tremolo-figure in the right hand.
 Supported by the authority of that unrivalled adept in things Beethovenian, Franz Liszt, we maintain, that
during the points of repose in the melodic course of the bass, the accompaniment-figure should assume the
form of 4 groups of 16th-notes, to be executed quietly, smoothly, and without accent: whereas, while the bass is rising or falling, the figure must form a group of six notes of *thematic* value:
etc. The abbreviations used by the author in his manuscript may be to blame for the un-
certainty.

a) These passages must be played with great buoyancy and fire, and, though each hand must bring out the figure allotted to it with all possible characteristic expression, their interwoven alternations should be so intimately combined that not the slightest hiatus may be perceptible.

a) Difficult as this passage is to execute — for dilettanti of the old-fashioned type — with the fingering given here (thumb on the black key "bb", it still, even when imperfectly executed, is preferable to the only apparent facilitation obtained by taking the dominant F with the thumb, which demands an agility scarcely to be expected from the player after the exertion caused by the preceding.

b) A material facilitation, however, especially for strongly marked accentuation, is obtained by allotting a fragment of the passage to the left hand.

a) "Sempre Pedale" is explicitly directed by the composer. D♭ and C, therefore, are to blend together; the resulting indistinctness is æsthetically justifiable.

b) The right hand must play its four strokes with such transparent delicacy, that the bass notes will be most impressive even to a comparatively unpractised ear.

c) Play the inner and lower parts of the accompaniment with equal force throughout.

d) The hands must alternate like two combattants in the violence of their strokes. But in the first two measures, a *sforzando* with the left hand on the first and third beats is still to be avoided, as prejudicial to the rhythmic interest and its intensification in the third measure.

a) The difficulty of connecting the accompaniment while the hands are crossed might perhaps be obviated by the following allotment:

b) Beware of a pleonastic *"ritardando"* in the last measure but one. The need of it has been sufficiently anticipated by the Author by transforming the quarter-notes in the bass into half-notes.

a) This movement is ordinarily played as much too fast as the Finale is taken too slow. But *"andante"* means *moving;* and, with *"con moto,"* even *flowing.* The addition, however, may also be understood here as meaning that a rigid adherence to the tempo throughout the movement should be avoided—— e. g., that perhaps the second Variation, and at any rate the third, may be slightly accelerated. But any unrestfulness in the several numbers would disturb the contemplative character which distinguishes this middle movement, and which demands a lofty simplicity of interpretation equally remote from emotional sentimentality and cool indifference.

b) The slurs added by the Editor are intended less to indicate the *legato,* which is here a matter of course, than to clearly set forth the proper phrasing of the melody. It is evident that the eighth-note b♭ in meas. 2 deserves stronger emphasis than the quarter-note b♭ in meas. 1; and that the b♭♭ in meas. 6 requires a similar accentuation—— the melody wanders over, as it were, into the bass. In the second part great attention must be paid to correct shading (precisely the same reading is necessary in Var. 2 and 3), and the structure of the period attentively analyzed; the "fore-phrase" has two parallel sections of two measures each, the "after-phrase" has four measures, and is to be played "in one breath."

c) For the better execution of the *legato,* divide the parts as follows:

d) Let the right hand play quite without expression—— mechanically, so to speak—— while strictly observing the time-value of each note; the left, on the contrary, very expressively, and *legatissimo.*

The player must rely on his touch to display the wondrous poetic beauty of this Variation, and to render it sufficiently euphonious without endeavoring to bemask the wierd harshnesses in the coincident progression of the parts.

a) This Variation would sound very dry, should the player not employ the peculiar pianoforte – effect obtained by treating the separate tones like sustained parts; purity of harmony must of course still be

preserved: etc.

a) The transition to a (but slightly) more animated tempo must be effected in the very beginning of this measure. The use of the pedal is permissible, in this and the preceding Variation, to an extent not interfering with distinctness. Do not play the figures with an extreme *legato;* what is called the "pearly" touch is peculiarly appropriate here. At the very beginning, the player was cautioned against an over-expressive delivery of the melody; strong emotion, but carefully kept within bounds, is fitting to the preceding Var. alone.

a) Play the highest parts *piano*, executing the bass in a *mezzo forte* such as a freely improvising violon-cellist would employ. The pianist should study the peculiar tone of the low violoncello-strings.

Allegro ma non troppo. ($\musNote = 132 - 138.$)

a) The last chord but one may be arpeggio'd very slowly and dreamily, the last must sound, above all things, energetic. The length of the hold depends upon the sonority of the instrument.

b) (notation) is the diminution of (notation), and must be executed with a consciousness of the rhythmic intensification of the emotion.

a) I owe this fingering, which has a singular look at first, but which the practical test of years has proved to be of unrivalled excellence, to my honored friend the music-teacher Franz Kroll of Berlin, whose editions of the classics have done so much for the instruction of artists and public alike. It fits the musical phrasing so perfectly, that by consistently carrying it out the entire movement might be transposed *all'im-provvista* into any other desired key. Without exactly repudiating the use of the thumb on C on the second beat, we must acknowledge that the passing-over of the third finger (as if with a spring) renders the needful accent less sharp, and—as only the practising player, not the reader, can convince himself— dismembers the whole phrase quite as little.

b) The 16th-note in the *auftakt* should be wellnigh conspicuously detached from the following quarter-note, whose time-value must not be curtailed.

c) The left hand should clearly phrase ♪♪♪ etc.

a) Bear in mind the last Note on the preceding page.

b) The melodic movement of the soprano ♪ is paralleled in this measure and the next by the ideal movement of the inner parts ♪, a point which the player should notice.

c) In this movement, one of the most passionate of all created by the composer, even the figuration must continually thrill and quiver with the liveliest agitation. In order to acquire sufficient strength to effect this, the player must study each single passage slowly, forcibly, and with most expressive accentuation. An actual *staccato* in its performance is of course impracticable, in view of the rapidity of the movement, but shun, when practising it, a *legato* touch detrimental to the individual animation of the separate tones. The tempestuous rising and falling runs for the left hand in the next 14 measures ought to be made the subject of very special study; during the points of rest in the right hand, in particular, the bass should continually occupy the listeners' attention. The most essential features in the shading are indicated by additional marks in the music.

a) This tremolo, of extreme difficulty for hands incapable of wide stretches, can be facilitated by no variant which would not produce disfigurement.

b) Imagine this plaintive motive in the left-hand inner parts:

c) The real melody lies in the soprano (right hand), and must not be obliterated by the figuration; its fluid state ought rather to intensify its incisiveness.

a) The counter-melody ![notation] requires very expressive delivery, and, as its appropriate dynamic shading is nearly opposed to that of the principal melody in the left hand, the hands must be trained to the utmost independence of each other.

b) The customary fingering, in which the accented G is taken with the thumb in both hands, is not "objectionable", but that of the Editor is better adapted to bring out the emotional imitation by both parts in the less accented notes as well.

c) It ought to be self-evident that the *sforzato* on the fourth eighth-note must not be transferred to the first in the next measure; and yet celebrated artists are frequently guilty of such amateurish liberties in public concerts, sometimes acting on the notion, that their variant is more in unison with "natural feeling."

d) Notice — in contrast with the preceding passages — the employment of the *major* **sixth** (instead of the *minor*) in the descending C-minor scale.

a¹) and a²) As the great composer uses all the arts of thematic work and imitative counterpoint solely for the purpose of intensifying the dramatic effect, so also should the player of his works make it a rule to accompany increased polyphony and complexity in the composition by enhanced agitation and dramatic spirit in the interpretation. All such contrapuntal dialogues between the hands ought therefore to be practised until their performance is not merely quite clear and correct, but likewise imbued with intensest psychic passion. __ The modification of the fingering at a²) for the principal theme is occasioned by the wide stretches required in the right-hand part.

a) This new motive begins on the *sf* quarter-note. First, 4 measures "solo"*(piano)*; then 4 measures "tutti"*(forte)*, in the key of the subdominant; then a repetition, in the tonic key, of this alternation be-tween *solo* and *tutti*. The rhythmical structure being so simple, it is surprising that the *forte*, assigned through carelessness (of the engraver?) to the first eighth-note of the measure where the right hand comes in with octaves, was allowed to pass uncorrected by the revisors of the new Complete Edition of Breitkopf and Härtel.

a) The Editor employs and recommends the following arrangement:

b) A hammering-out of the next eight measures in an undiscriminating *fortissimo* would be as unlovely in point of euphony as unsuited to the passionate undulation of the bass (which must predominate). Hence the added shading.

c) In this passage bear in mind the thematic significance of the first 4 notes, and play "imitatively" (of different instruments).

d) A (possibly indispensable) facilitation would be, to play only the first 2 notes with the left hand, the next 5 with the right, and then to take the final note (first eighth-note in next meas.) with the forefinger of the left.

a) This chord should be played with an extremely soft, "velvety" touch, which is promoted by a non-employment of the thumb.

b) By means of the fingering given here the entrance of the second beat marks itself, and no more forcibly than is exactly demanded; whereas by using the thumb such delicate accents are apt to be made coarser. Play the new counter-motive in the right hand with the utmost emotional expression.

a) The repetition of the bass note in each new measure, instead of at the beginning of every other measure as before, is indubitably owing to a misunderstanding of some abbreviation employed by the Author in his manuscript. Not on account of technical inconvenience, but on account of the æsthetic inelegance resulting from the interruption of the continuous undulatory movement by this repetition, does the Editor reject this pseudo-"classic" misprint.

a) Excepting the case in the Finale of the C-minor Symphony (first part), the Editor knows no more unjustifiable compulsion to repetition than this. The whole poem presses to a close; the player, who thus far has striven with all the technical and mental energy at his command to fulfil his task, must now be so near exhaustion, as to be obliged to muster his entire remaining strength in order to meet the demands of the Coda —demands hardly to be over-estimated. If he obeys the repeat, his work will be inferior to the first time (unless he unduly saved his strength before); on the listener the repetition may make a didactic, but in no case an artistico-plastic impression; therefore, let reverence for an extrinsic matter of inattention on the Master's part be saved up for private practice, in which the reproductive musician must always be able to accomplish at least twice as much as is required of him at a public concert.

a) The two first strokes must always be somewhat detached from what follows; a very moderate, short accent on the first eighth-note in the third and fifth measures (in the second part, where the 8-measure period expands to one of 10 measures, this also applies to the seventh) will add materially to the distinctness of the melody.

b) If a further acceleration be observed from this point to the end, it will be quite in keeping with the continuous pressing toward the close.

c) In consequence of special practice, the Editor finds it easy to pass the thumb under the little finger; or the latter over the thumb. To the fingering ⟨figure⟩ he is opposed on principle, as the fluency of the phrase and the accentuation of the first tone must suffer from it. Thumb on E and G is awkward, as hampering the motion of the already tired fingers. But B♭ might again be taken with the thumb, provided that appropriate technical exercises had been practised beforehand.

a) Sound *C-F* shrill like a trumpet-call here; at b) like a drum-beat.

BEETHOVEN
his greatest
PIANO SOLOS

VOLUME II

Compiled by Robert Kail

Copyright©MCMLXXVIII by Copa Publishing Co.

Ashley Dealers Service, Inc.,

SEVEN VARIATIONS
on "My Country 'Tis of Thee" (God Save the King)

4

VAR. II.

VAR. III.

6

VAR. VII.

Five Variations on
RULE BRITANNIA

VAR. I.

14

VAR. III.

TWO CHROMATIC PRELUDES
(Through All Major Tonalities)
(Op. 39)

POLONAISE
(Op. 89)

Alla Polacca, vivace.

VARIATIONS AND FUGUE
(on themes from the Eroica Symphony)

Canone all'ottava.

VAR.VII.

VAR.VIII.

Allegro con brio.

FINALE.
Alla Fuga.

SIX BAGATELLES
(Op. 126)

La seconda parte due volte.

No. 2.

Andante.
Cantabile e grazioso.

№ 3.

Presto.

N.º 4.

Quasi allegretto.

№ 5.

MINUET AND TRIO

Moderato.

68

SIX MINUETS

Nº 1.

Men. da capo.

N.º 2.

Men. da capo.

Nᵒ 4.

Trio.

Men. da capo.

Nº 5.

Trio.

Menf. da capo.

N°. 6.

Men. da capo.

PRELUDE

RONDO

78

TWELVE VARIATIONS
(on a Minuet by Haibl)

VAR. II.

VAR. III.

dolce

ligato

SONATA IN F MINOR
(Composed at the age of 11)

Larghetto maestoso.

Allegro assai.

SIX EASY VARIATIONS

VAR. II.

VAR. III.

VAR. VI.

SONATINA IN G

ROMANZE.

AN EASY SONATA

Adagio.

THE DIABELLI VARIATIONS
(33 Variations on a Waltz by Diabelli)

Allegro ma non troppo e serioso.

VAR.VI.

Un poco più allegro.

VAR.VII.

122

130

132

VAR. XXIV.

Fughetta.
Andante.

una corda, sempre ligato

134

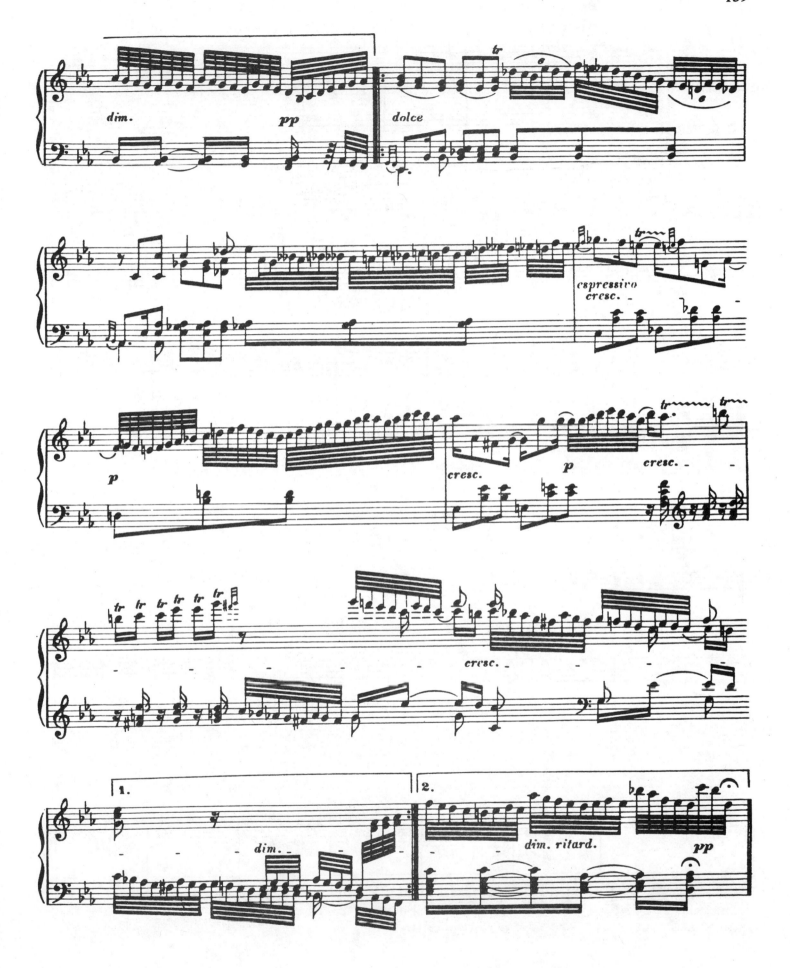

Tempo di Minuetto moderato (ma non tirarsi dietro)(aber nicht schleppend.)

SIX FOLK DANCES

SEVEN FOLK DANCES

Nº 7.

Coda.

SIX VARIATIONS
(on the "Turkish March")

158